Made in West Africa

MADE IN WEST AFRICA

by Christine Price

illustrated with photographs and drawings

E. P. DUTTON & CO., INC. NEW YORK

To Jeannette Mirsky

LIBRARY OF CONGRESS CATALOGING IN PUBLICATION DATA

Price, Christine   Made in West Africa

SUMMARY: Discusses the influences of African customs,
history, and geography upon art in West Africa. Includes
dress, textiles, jewelry, metal sculpture, carving, masks,
and pottery.

1. Negro arts—Africa, West—Juvenile literature.
[1. Negro arts—Africa, West. 2. Arts—Africa] I. Title.
NX589.P54 700'.966 74-4202 ISBN 0-525-34400-4

Published simultaneously in Canada by Clarke,
Irwin & Company Limited, Toronto and Vancouver
Printed in the U.S.A.   First Edition
10 9 8 7 6 5 4 3 2 1

Frontispiece: Egungun society mask.
Yoruba, Nigeria. (For back view of
mask, see page v.)

Author's Note

Most of the works of art shown in this book cannot be identified by the names of the artists who created them. We can name the country that the art comes from and the group of people for whom it was made. We can tell by the style of work whether the artist was Yoruba or Ashanti, Baule or Dan. But we can seldom name the artists themselves until we come to those who are working today, and especially to the contemporary sculptors, painters, and printmakers who have broken away from the traditional styles of the past.

Yet traditional African art, no less than the new art of today, is the work of individual men and women. Outstanding artists were—and still are—well known among their own people, and each has added to the richness and variety of African art.

In this book we can only begin to explore West African arts of the past and present. Having made this first step, I hope that some readers will want to go further. Among the sources of the illustrations, listed in detail at the end of the book, are museums where great collections of African art can be seen.

My own exploration of African art could not have been made without the generous help of many people, both in America and in West Africa, and to all of them I owe a debt of gratitude.

I am most grateful to the following for supplying me with photographs and giving me permission to use them in the book:

The American Museum of Natural History, New York; William

Bascom; The Trustees of the British Museum, London; The Brooklyn Museum, New York; Kevin Carroll; Philip Dark; Henry Drewal; Federation of Nigeria, Information Service; The Ghana Information Services; Aldo Merusi; Marshall W. Mount; The Museum of Primitive Art, New York; Sandi Olivo; Marc Pevar; The Smithsonian Institution, Washington, D.C.; Robert F. Thompson; The UCLA Museum of Cultural History, Los Angeles; The United Nations; The University Museum, University of Pennsylvania; Frank Willett.

My special thanks are due to Dr. Philip Allen and Professor Frank Willett for reading the manuscript of the book and making many corrections and criticisms. Their help and encouragement were invaluable.

C. P.

Above and at right: Ivory horsemen.
Yoruba, Nigeria.

Contents

River Niger

NIGER

MALI

UPPER VOLTA

GUINEA

BAGA

NIGERIA

SIERRA
LEONE

DAHOMEY

River Niger

SHERBRO

IVORY COAST

GHANA

TOGO

Old Oyo

River

MENDE

YORUBA

DAN

GURO

ASHANTI

Abomey

Ife

LIBERIA

NGERE

BAULE

FON

Ibadan

AGNI

Kumasi

Benin City

Monrovia

EDO

IBO

Abidjan

Accra

Cotonou

Lagos

IJO

IBIBIO

Brass

Map of West Africa

Made in West Africa

1

The Land,
the People,
and the Arts

In Africa art has always been a part of life. The famous masks and wood sculptures of the lands of West Africa belong to the whole pattern of West African arts, all woven together in the lives of the people. You cannot separate the art of woodcarving from pottery, weaving, or metalwork. And all these arts—things that we can see and touch—are bound up with music and storytelling, poetry and dance.

African arts are arts of action. Poetry is for singing, music is for dancing. Stories can be told in movement and song, with rhythmic chanting and clapping.

The act of making a piece of sculpture, whether it is molded from clay or cut from a log of wood, may be more important to the African artist than the finished work itself. And what he makes is not something to be looked at in silence and awe.

Left: Animal mask. Ibo, Nigeria.
Above: Seated figure. Baule,
Ivory Coast.

Carved figures may be carried, swinging and swaying, in a festival procession, and wooden masks come alive in the dance.

We cannot explore these arts with our eyes alone. All the senses must come into play.

The African mask that hangs on a wall is cold and dead. It should crown the costume that covers the dancer from head to foot. The mask must move, as the dancer moves, to the music of instruments and singers. And sometimes the dancer, his body hidden by mask and costume, seems to be changed from a man into a spirit, a mysterious being with power over the lives of the people.

Left: Gelede dance at Ajilete, in southwestern Nigeria.
Above: Miniature brass figure of masked dancer. Baule, Ivory Coast.

3

4

The awesome Nimba mask of the Baga people comes forth in majesty to bring fruitfulness to the farmers' fields. The masks of the Poro secret society dance to the drums at the initiation of young boys, the great ceremony that marks their entry into manhood. The Gelede masks, nimble and quick-stepping, dance to control witchcraft and evil, and their design is supposed to be pleasing to potential witches in the audience. Almost anything—from a tree to a snake or a sewing machine—may be carved on top of the head, but the basic form of the Gelede mask, and the way it is worn, are set by tradition. The carvers of masks must always be guided by the work of their forefathers and the customs of their people.

Left: Nimba mask. Baga, Guinea.
Above left: Poro society masks.
Ngere, Ivory Coast.
Above: Gelede mask. Yoruba, Nigeria.
When mask was worn, real palm fronds
were placed in the top of the carved
palm tree.

5

The arts of West Africa reach back far into the past. Long before white men landed on the Guinea Coast, there were artists and craftsmen at work in towns and villages in the deep forest and in the grasslands bordering the Sahara Desert. Great kings ruled in West Africa, and empires rose and fell there hundreds of years ago. The people belonged to many different groups with their own languages, customs, and beliefs, and their own forms of art.

Their ways of living, and their arts, were shaped by the land they lived on. Along the hot, low-lying coast, fringed with mangrove swamps and white sandy beaches, there were villages of fishermen. Inland, the people lived mainly by farming. Where the forest spread over the earth like a dark green blanket, the farmers cut down the trees and burned off the undergrowth to make their fields.

Above right: Stone head. Bulom or Sherbro, Sierra Leone.
Above: Carved wooden pulley from a loom. Guro, Ivory Coast.

Fishing village of Ganvie, Dahomey.
Houses stand on stilts in a coastal
lagoon and people travel by canoe.

In the towns that clustered around the palaces of kings there were many artists and craftsmen. The finest of them produced the royal arts that only kings might own and use. Village artists usually worked as farmers as well. When the harvest was gathered in and there was food for everyone, they had time to perfect their skills.

The land gave the artists a rich choice of materials to work with. Besides wood for the carver, the forest offered raffia and other fibers; leaves and bark and vegetable dyes. Hide, bone, and ivory came from the bodies of animals. The earth itself gave clay for the potter, stone for the sculptor, and iron and bright gold for the mysterious art of the smith.

Tiny brass figures of a king and his
retainers. Fon, Dahomey.

8

Some of the West African peoples were more gifted in music, dance, and song than in the art of making things. But everywhere the work of artists and craftsmen was needed, whether they made household pots or beaded crowns for kings. Art was as necessary as food and drink.

Bronze horsemen. Benin kingdom, Nigeria.

9

Works of art could also serve as records of history and tradition. Few peoples in West Africa had written languages before
the white men came. Their histories and ancient wisdom, passed
down by word of mouth, were recorded in the artists' language
of pictures and symbols.

Royal arts could tell of the mighty deeds of kings, and even
simple everyday things could be made to carry a message. The
decorations carved on a calabash spoke of love, and the patterns
on a cloth could teach useful lessons in living.

Yoruba potter at work in Ilorin,
Nigeria.

Art spoke also of the gods the people worshiped, and of the ancestors who had lived long ago and still watched over their children's children. Masks and carved figures were links with the spirit-world, which was as real to the people as the red earth of their fields.

Today, in the countries of West Africa, many old customs and beliefs have died away. Old arts have died with them. Traditional wood sculptures and masks have no meaning for many Africans, for these things belong to times and ways of living that are gone forever. New artists are creating new forms of art that express their own feelings about life in modern Africa.

Yet some of the old arts are still alive and strong. Artists and craftsmen are still working in the ways of their forefathers, using the same simple tools to make the things their people need. We find them at work in modern cities, in quiet villages, and in old towns governed by traditional chiefs and kings.

Duga, a Yoruba woodcarver. Meko, Nigeria.

Our journey in search of art, old and new, will take us into the rain forest and along its borders, through the lands that once were divided among four great kingdoms—the empires of the Ashanti, the Fon people of Dahomey, the Yoruba, and the Edo people of Benin.

A good place to begin our travels is in the crowded market of a West African city. The sun blazes down on tin-roofed stalls and teeming streams of people who have come from miles around to buy and sell. There is a babel of voices as the market women haggle over their trading among many-colored heaps of fruits and vegetables. We jump out of the way to let a line of women sail by with easy strides carrying baskets of yams on their heads. Past the foodstuff market, we come to the stalls where they sell bright enamelware, plastic goods, traveling bags, and shiny shoes. Then we find people selling things they have made, things that may come from distant villages known for their arts and skills. There are farm tools of handwrought iron, baskets, decorated calabashes, and fine pottery. We see art all around us, starting with the dress of the people who buy and sell.

Here are the arts that are a part of life!

Left: Market at Kumasi, Ghana.
Above: Epa mask, with carving of a mother and child. Yoruba, Nigeria.

The Textile Arts

Even in a crowded market the women are elegantly dressed. They carry themselves proudly, as people do who are used to bearing loads on their heads. Among Yoruba women, the traditional color for wrapped skirts, loose blouses, and head-ties is blue, the cool blue of indigo. In the market of a Yoruba town we find rolls of blue cloth for sale. If we stop to admire the patterns, we are surrounded by the women who dye and sell the cloth. Each one declares the beauty of her cloths and shakes them out for us to see.

Left: Woman's loom. Ososo, village northeast of Benin, Nigeria.

In this tie-dyed cloth, the small circular designs were made by pinching up tiny bits of the material and tying them with raffia before dyeing. For the larger designs tucks were made in the cloth and tightly sewn. When the woman dipped the white cloth in her big earthenware dye-pot, the indigo dye could not soak into the tied and sewn parts. These showed up white after the cloth was dried and the stitching and raffia were taken out. Then another dipping stained the white designs a soft pale blue.

Each pattern has a name. The cross-shaped pattern in the center of this cloth is called The Meeting Place of Roads, and the spiral that looks like a string of beads is Welcome to the Masquerade!

There are also resist-dyed cloths. Here the patterns were painted on, either freehand or using a metal stencil. A feather or a rib of palm leaf served as a brush, and the paint was a mixture of alum and starchy cassava that protected the cloth from the dye. The patterns came out white when the paint was scraped off after the cloth had been dipped in the indigo. We find geometric patterns, figures of men and animals, or letters of the alphabet. Different combinations of designs give each cloth its name. One is called All the Birds Are Here, and another, We Enjoy Ibadan.

The big city of Ibadan in Nigeria is one of the centers for the dyeing of these blue *adire* cloths. Many of them are sold in other countries of West Africa, far from the land of the Yoruba people. The dyers of adire cloth work with machine-made cotton material, but handwoven cloths can also be found in the market.

Weaving was a West African craft long before the coming of the white men. Both men and women are weavers, but they use different kinds of looms. The woman's loom is upright and produces a wide strip of fabric. This may be plain-colored, striped, or worked in rich woven patterns.

The man's loom is narrow and horizontal, producing a long thin band of material only a few inches wide. These woven strips are sewn together, side by side, to make large cloths or tailored clothes—tunics, gowns, and trousers.

Man's loom. Dahomey.

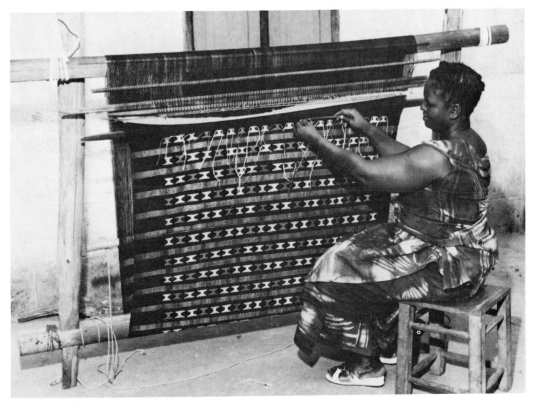

Women's looms. Nigeria.

Yoruba men dress with as much flair and brilliance as their wives. A man walks with dignity in the long flowing gown called *agbada*, and it swirls about him when his feet move in the small intricate steps of Yoruba dance.

Embroidery is used to decorate men's clothes in Yorubaland and among the Fon people of Dahomey. The elegant suit from Dahomey (right) is embroidered and also worked in appliqué. Appliqué fish on the trousers suggest that these clothes may have belonged to the last great king of the Fon people, Behanzin, whose insignia was the shark. Behanzin ruled over the old kingdom of Dahomey at the end of the nineteenth century until he was defeated by the French and sent into exile.

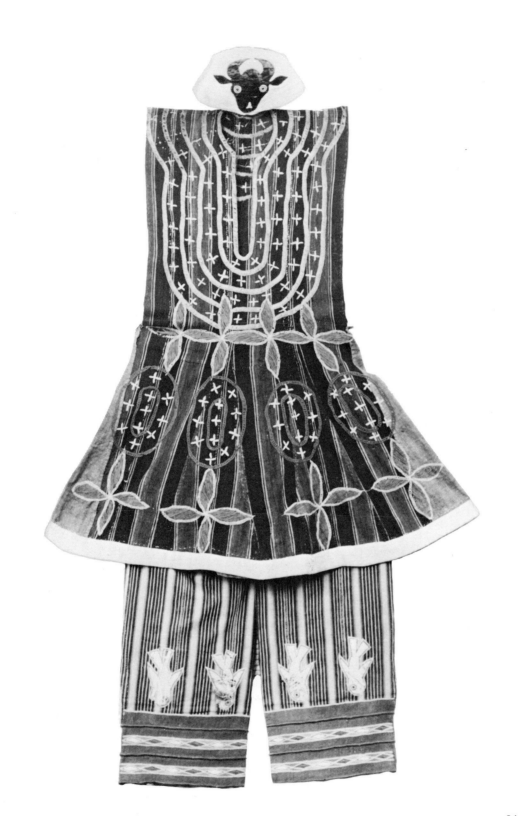

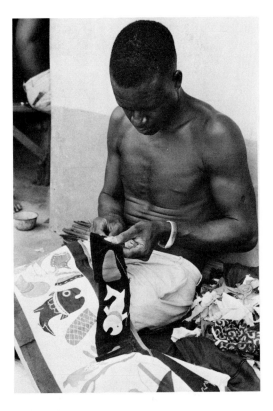

Appliqué work in Dahomey was far more than a way of decorating clothes. It was an important royal art. The men who did the appliqué worked in the palace of the king at Abomey, along with goldsmiths, brass-casters, weavers, and carvers of wood and ivory. The appliqué workers would decorate tents and banners and the state umbrellas carried in royal processions. Above all, they made the appliqué cloths that told in pictures the history of the kingdom.

Today, although the palace at Abomey is a museum, men still sit in a quiet courtyard there and sew the appliqué cloths, as they used to do when they worked for the king. But now they sell their work to anyone who will buy.

The storytelling cloths are wall hangings, with the figures cut out and stitched onto a background of black or gold.

Here is a cloth with the symbols of all the kings, from the founding of the kingdom in the early seventeenth century to its downfall in the time of Behanzin.

An appliqué worker at Abomey sews
the cut-out symbols onto the cloth.

The ship, symbol of King Agadja, recalls a turning point in the history of Dahomey. King Agadja extended his empire down to the coast and was the first of the kings to meet the white men who landed there.

The white traders called this land the Slave Coast, and the rulers in Abomey grew rich on the slave trade. Armed with guns from the white men, the armies of Dahomey fought long wars against the Yoruba kingdom of Oyo to the east. Grim memories of those wars are recorded on the appliqué cloths, showing Yoruba prisoners led away to slaughter or to slavery.

One of those who died was a Yoruba ruler, captured by the great King Glele, and put to death by Behanzin, Glele's successor.

Figures from the appliqué cloth on page 22 (top to bottom): Ship of King Agadja; Lion of King Glele; Yoruba king, hanged by King Behanzin.

24

West of Dahomey was the kingdom of the Ashanti. Here the royal artists worked for the *Asantehene*, the supreme ruler of the state. They included weavers of the famous *kente* cloth, which is still made and worn as the national dress of modern Ghana.

Men's dress. Ashanti, Ghana.

Kente is woven in long narrow strips on a man's loom. When the pieces are sewn together to make a large cloth, the designs are combined in a brilliant checkered pattern. Originally the threads of bright silk used in the weaving were unraveled from European cloth, bought from white traders. In the past kente cloth was made strictly for the royal house. Ashanti kings and queens had their own personal designs. All new patterns invented by the weavers belonged to the Asantehene, who might keep them for his own use or give them to the men and women of the court.

One of the most famous patterns, only woven by master weavers, was called My Skill Is Exhaused—My Ideas Have Run Out. Another was called The Sky God's Arch (The Rainbow), and another, in fresh green and yellow, was The Tender Leaf of the Cocoyam.

The village of Bonwire near Kumasi, the capital of the old Ashanti kingdom, was the original home of the kente weavers. There the art was passed down from father to son. Nowadays there are kente weavers in other towns, but those in Bonwire still consider themselves the best.

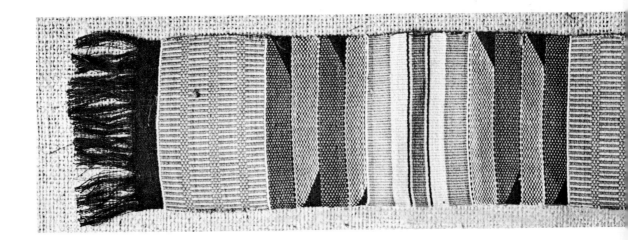

Left: Part of a large kente cloth, made from many strips sewn together, Ashanti, Ghana.
Above: Single strip of kente cloth, woven of cotton and silk in red, black, gold, and green.

27

Another village near Kumasi specializes in the making of *adinkra* cloth. Adinkra means "farewell," and this cotton cloth, decorated with hand-printed patterns, was formerly worn only for funerals.

The big newly printed cloths of white, green, red, and russet-orange hang out along the roadside in Ntonso, the cloth-printers' village. Blue smoke rises from the outdoor fires where the black printing ink is prepared. Pieces of fibrous inner bark from the *badie* tree are boiled in water for half a day. Then the liquid is reboiled with lumps of iron slag until it thickens.

The printing stamps are skillfully carved from small pieces of the hard skin of a calabash. Three pointed slivers of wood, stuck in the back of the stamp and tied together with thread, make a convenient handle. The printer squats beside the cloth, which is spread on a low padded surface. Using several different stamps, he dips each one into the thick black ink and prints the designs swiftly, close together, until the whole cloth is covered.

Adinkra stamps. The center one has a handle. The designs and their meanings (left to right): Defiance— I am not afraid of you; the power of God; pattern derived from a court hairstyle.

Besides being beautiful to look at when it is worn as a graceful draped costume, adinkra cloth has much to say to those who know the meaning of the patterns. Reading the message of the adinkra stamps, we learn some of the wisdom of the Ashanti people: their patience and fortitude; their faith in the Supreme God, Nyame; their loyalty to family and king. While men and women both wear the cloth, some designs are only for men, like the crossed swords that stand for bravery in battle.

A boy prints a large cloth with stamps like those at the left.

29

It is said that the adinkra patterns and the art of cloth-printing came from the country west of the Ashanti kingdom, now called the Ivory Coast. A king of the Ivory Coast named Adinkra was defeated and killed in battle by the Ashanti at the beginning of the nineteenth century. He was wearing a printed cloth at the time, and his son, who was taken prisoner, revealed to the Ashanti the secrets of cloth-printing.

The Ashanti went to war against Adinkra because he had dared to make a copy of their sacred Golden Stool. After Adinkra's defeat and death, the royal goldsmiths of the Ashanti melted down the false golden stool and made it into two portrait masks of the dead king. These were hung, upside down, on either side of the throne of the Asantehene, adding their brightness to the golden splendor of his court.

Man's cloth, printed with a crossed-sword design on a red background.

Adinkra designs and their meanings:

1   Unity—offend no one without cause

2   Forgiveness—turn the other cheek

3   Safety and security at home

4   Moon and star—faithfulness

5   The king's eye—the king sees all

6   Heart—patience and endurance

7   Turn back—you can undo your mistakes

8   Star, child of the heavens—I depend on
    God alone

9   Everlasting life

10 Link or chain—people are linked in
    life and death

The Ashanti kingdom was well named the Gold Coast by European traders. Gold dust and nuggets of gold were to be found there. Threads of gold were woven into the brilliant kente cloth, and nowhere was golden jewelry more wonderfully made than in the land of the Ashanti.

Two crocodiles with one stomach (see pages 34–35).

Metalwork,
Ivory,
and Beads

The miniature mask, a few inches high, was a favorite form of gold jewelry. It would hang on a man's chest, gleaming against his dark skin or the bright folds of his cloth.

The mask shown above was made by a goldsmith of the Baule people, neighbors and relatives of the Ashanti, living in the southern part of the Ivory Coast. The Baule and the Ashanti both value gold above all other metals, and in the past, besides making gold jewelry, they used gold dust as money.

When a man wanted to buy something, he carried a bag containing a little brass box of gold dust, a set of brass goldweights, and a scale. The goldsmiths themselves made the weights, with all the skill and care they used when making jewelry.

Left: Small bronze masks, 18th century, to be worn as ornaments at the waist. Benin, Nigeria.

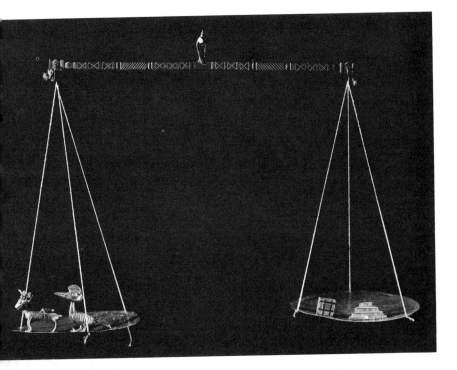

At first the weights were made in simple, geometric shapes. Later they took the form of animals and people, plants and insects, or furnishings of the royal palace—stools, state swords, guns, and drums. Many of the weights illustrated proverbs and wise sayings.

Two birds facing each other and fighting with their beaks bear the message that a battle of words injures no one. Several birds climbing up a tree trunk represent the Ashanti version of "Birds of a feather flock together."

A chief seated on his throne points out the people's need for good leadership, while a hunter attacked by a leopard is a grim reminder not to bite off more than one can chew. The two crocodiles, who share the same stomach but still fight over their food, poke fun at anyone who is greedy and wants too much for himself.

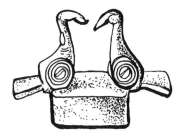

Scales and weights for gold dust. Ashanti, Ghana.

*Goldweights and box for gold dust,
made of brass. Ashanti.*

35

The old method of casting jewelry and goldweights, the lost-wax process, is still used today in West Africa by makers of fine metalwork.

The goldsmith first models the piece of sculpture or jewelry in wax. He makes the model solid if it is as small as a goldweight. For a larger sculpture he shapes the wax over a core of clay.

The delicate spiral forms that we often see in Baule and Ashanti work are made from slender threads of soft wax rolled out on a smooth board. Looking closely at the birds perched on this little brass box, we find that their folded wings are represented by pairs of these tiny spirals.

The finished model is painted with a thin watery mixture of fine clay, then coated with layers of coarse clay to make the mold for casting. When the mold is heated, the wax melts and runs out through a hole left for this purpose. Then molten metal is poured into the mold to fill the space left by the wax.

Brass box for gold dust. Ashanti.

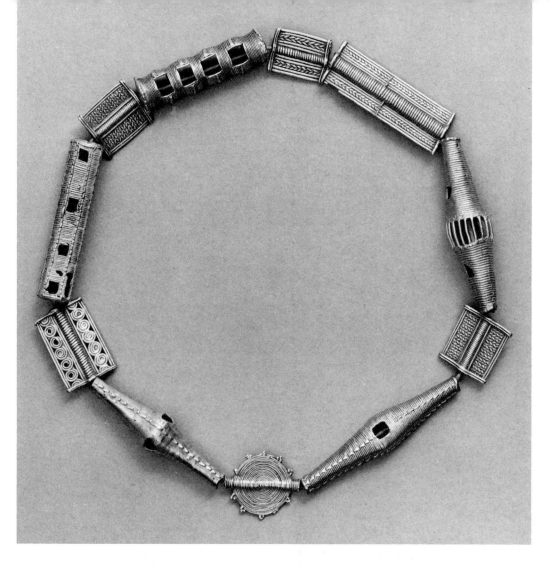

The Ashanti or Baule goldsmith uses another method of filling the mold when he is casting a small object. He puts pieces of cold metal into a clay crucible and fastens this to the bottom of the mold. The whole thing, thickly covered with clay, is then set in hot charcoal. When the metal has melted, the mold is lifted and turned upside down so that the liquid metal can pour down inside it.

After the goldsmith judges that the metal is cool and hard, he breaks open the clay, takes out the casting, and smooths and finishes it with a file.

Gold necklace. Ashanti.

Ashanti gold jewelry, still made in designs that were popular a hundred years ago, is widely sold and worn throughout West Africa. Among the Ashanti in the past, only the Asantehene and the high chiefs were entitled to wear gold jewelry, and it is still an important part of the trappings of royalty. Besides bracelets, pendants, and necklaces of gold beads, Ashanti rulers wear hats, crowns, and even sandals encrusted with gold.

Ruler enthroned with his family and retainers. Ghana.

But not all peoples valued gold as highly as the Ashanti did. In the kingdom of Benin, the Edo people considered brass or bronze to be of greater worth, and they treasured ivory as a material for making jewelry. The bronze-casters of Benin worked exclusively for the *Oba,* the all-powerful king whose vast palace stood—and still stands—in the center of Benin City.

His empire had close ties with the Yoruba kingdom to the west. The first Oba of Benin was a Yoruba prince who came from the royal city of Ife not later than the twelfth century. And it was an Ife artist who went to Benin in the fourteenth century to teach the metalworkers the art of bronze-casting by the lost-wax method. This man, Igueghae, was remembered ever afterwards as the patron of the bronze-casters, and they keep a shrine dedicated to him in Benin today.

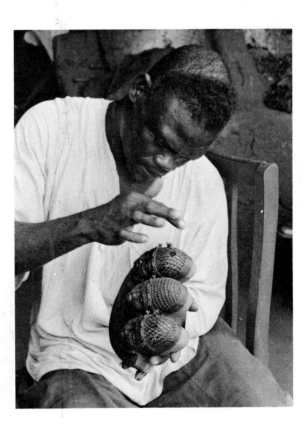

Brass-casters in Benin still use the lost-wax method. A master craftsman finishes a wax model for casting.

39

Top: Benin brass-casters, after
firing clay molds and draining the
wax out, bury molds in earth. Molten
metal is poured into molds from a
crucible held in the tongs.
At left: Ornamental hip mask made
in Benin in 1959. At right: Similar
mask made in Benin about 1850.

These bronze masks, and the two on page 32, show how well the men of Benin learned their art from the Yoruba master. The Oba would wear small masks like these in sets of two or three, fastened at his waist. On festival days he was a magnificent figure, dressed in layer upon layer of rich material reaching to the ground, a helmet on his head, and a high collar of coral beads around his neck. On his arms were broad bracelets of precious ivory. One of these bracelets, a miracle of miniature workmanship, has a carving of the Oba himself, not as a man but as a god whom the people worshiped.

Ivory armlet, inlaid with bronze, made of two cylinders carved from a single tusk. Hidden inner cylinder has elephant head design. Benin, about 1550.

The splendor of the Oba's court in the fifteenth century astonished the Portuguese, the first Europeans to find their way to Benin. When they began to trade with Benin and were often seen in the city, their images appeared in the art of the metalworkers and ivory carvers. An ivory mask, one of the masterpieces of Benin art, is bordered by a row of capped and bearded heads, unmistakably white men.

Although the ivory carvers were not restricted to working for the Oba, he gave them plenty to do. One tusk from every elephant killed in the kingdom had to be presented to him, and his ivory carvings were considered to be his greatest treasures.

Benin ivories: Mask, from the early 16th century, was worn at the waist or as a pendant.
Right: Small leopard with metal spots was worn on the Oba's forearm.

Yoruba craftsmen were also skilled in ivory carving. The rich design of this bracelet, similar to the one worn by the Oba, includes the figure of a Yoruba god-king in his beaded crown.

A high crown covered with beads is the sign of Yoruba kingship, and beaded crowns are still worn by the most important rulers in Yorubaland. The people say that this custom goes back to the time when the world was made by the god Oduduwa, who was the first ruler of Ife. He crowned his sixteen sons with beaded crowns and sent them away from Ife to rule over separate states, although some say his sons stole the crowns when their father was old and blind.

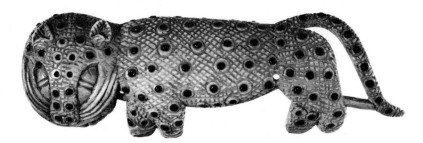

*Yoruba beaded royal crown, late
19th or early 20th century.*

44

Among the Yoruba, beadwork can only be used to make holy things, connected with kings or gods. The craftsmen who make the crowns build up the design by stitching single strands of white or colored beads onto a frame of wickerwork and cloth. The watchful face of Oduduwa is worked on the front of the crown, while a veil of beads hangs down to hide the face of the king. The crown itself is believed to act as a guardian against evil, and no king with evil in his heart may wear it.

A crown like the one at left is worn on state occasions when the king comes out of his palace to appear before his people. He is surrounded by the prominent members of the royal household. The king's drummers are there with the players of the great calabash rattles called *shekere*.

Art and music come together in the thrilling rhythms of drums and rattles, the glow of many colors in robes and draperies, and the glint of sunshine on jewelry and on the awesome beaded crown. The rattle players shake their shekere between their hands, beat upon them, and send them spinning into the air like balloons. Each rattle is clothed in strings of white cowrie shells that strike against the hard skin of the calabash with a strident sound. Even the humble calabash has been turned into a work of art! The African artist does not need gold or rich materials to make something beautiful, and his simplest arts can be as fine as all the jewelry in the palace.

Decorated
Calabashes

Calabashes play an important part in the varied music of West Africa. They serve as rattles, large and small, and with the addition of a skin drumhead, they become fat round calabash drums. They are also resonators for xylophones, hanging underneath the wooden keys, and sound boxes for stringed instruments.

But the most common use for calabashes is as household pots, dishes, and bowls. Before the coming of enamelware pots and pans, calabashes were essential in every West African household, and they still have many uses.

Like other gourds, they grow on a trailing plant. To make a calabash container, the ripe fruit is soaked in water until the seeds and pulp have rotted and can be scraped out. The calabash can be cut in various ways, depending on the shape one needs.

Far left: Gambian musician plays 21-stringed kora. Sound box is a calabash with leather stretched tightly over it.
Left and top: Ghanaian musicians with xylophone and calabash drum.

47

When the skin has been thoroughly dried, it is ready for decorating, a craft that is usually done by men. The dry skin is a warm yellow color that darkens with age and use, but it can be stained rosy red, dark blue, orange, or reddish brown. The smooth surface can be carved, scraped, or engraved, or black patterns can be burnt into it with a hot iron point.

This Yoruba carver, using a few simple tools, cuts his geometric design deep into the skin of the calabash. He makes no mark to guide his hand, working only by eye and the skill of long practice. If we compare his finished carving with a calabash from Nigeria that was carved a hundred years ago (page 50), we see how little the style of work has changed.

Above: The tools of Isola, a Yoruba calabash carver.
Above and at right: Two stages of Isola's work on the decoration of a calabash bowl.

Many Nigerian calabashes are darkly stained so that the designs appear black against a white, scraped background. This long thin one (two views are shown here), meant to hold henna for dyeing the fingernails, is the right shape for a woman to thrust her hand inside. The narrow opening grips her forearm, and she can go about her work while wearing the calabash on one hand.

In Dahomey a decorated calabash is the traditional present from a young man to the girl he wants to marry. Each of the designs represents a proverb, and if the proverbs are correctly understood, the lid of the calabash can be "read" like a love letter (page 52).

51

1   The snake design says: "Even if a serpent attacked you, I would cut off its head. And so would I kill any rival for your love!"

2   The curly-tailed chameleon says: "Mawa-Lisu (the moon goddess and sun god) will see that all goes well and the marriage takes place."

3   The Go bird says: "It is as easy for the fish to go into the big beak of the Go as for a man to take the woman who loves him."

4   The eyes say: "Let your heart be soft so that my eyes may always gaze at you."

5   The cross-shaped design says: "By the grace of Mawu, we will do what we want!"

Another calabash from Dahomey was found in the fishing village of Ganvie, which stands on stilts in a coastal lagoon (page 7). Carvings of canoes adorn the lower half, and on the lid are large fishes nibbling water weeds.

Side by side with the household calabashes, decorated or plain, the women of West Africa have earthenware pots for cooking and for storing food and water. Pottery-making is an ancient art in Africa, and the potters are almost always women, perhaps because from the beginning women have known best what pots the housewife needed.

The Art of
the Potter

The village potters of West Africa do not use the wheel for shaping their pots. The bottom of a large broken pot, set on the ground, will often serve as a base for working on a new lump of clay. The woman hollows out the center of the clay and pulls up the sides. Then she builds the walls of the pot to the height she wants by adding coils of clay, rolled out between the palms of her hands.

This potter in a village near Benin has almost finished shaping the rounded body of the water vessel she is making. She closes in the top to leave a hole for the mouth. As she begins to make the lip for the mouth of the pot, she stands up and walks around her work, keeping it perfectly circular. Before the pot is fired, she cuts and presses a pattern into the smooth body with little pieces of carved wood or plaited fiber.

Far left: Potter at work in village of Use, near Benin, Nigeria.
Left: Water vessel from Ghana in form of an animal, probably a rhinoceros.

We see a quite different form of decoration on this Ibo pot, made in the East-Central State of Nigeria. Here the rhythmic molded design, standing out from the body, has been painted dark brown against a background of orange. Although some pottery is polished, no glazes are used and there is no kiln for firing. When the pots have dried in the sun, they are fired in an open wood fire. Then the finished pots are carried off on the women's heads and taken to market, which often means a hot dusty walk of many miles.

Pot with molded ornament. Ibo, Nigeria.

*Above: Same potter of Use, shaping
the mouth of the pot.
Left: Her work in its final form,
with decoration.*

Skilled potters also make ceremonial vessels that are not found for sale in the market with the household wares.

The Ashanti "family pot" is for ceremonies after a funeral. The relatives of the dead person shave off their hair, put all the clippings into one of these vessels, and leave it near the grave in the "place of pots," together with a sacrifice of food.

Above right: Small red pottery bowl. Man, Ivory Coast.
Above: Ashanti "family pot"
(Abusua Kuruwa). Ghana.

A potter of Dahomey shapes the walls of a large water vessel.

The handsome old "jawbone pot" was made to hold the wine that is poured as an offering over the sacred Golden Stool of the Ashanti. Its smooth finish and formal decoration are a contrast to the lively art of an Ibo potter, from a village on the west bank of the River Niger.

"Jawbone pot." Ashanti, Ghana.

The little sculptured figures of men and women seem to sprout from the top of this bowl, which was used at the end of the nineteenth century in the worship of Ifijioku, the Yam Spirit. This spirit was vitally important to the villagers, for she watched over the farmers' crops of yams and granted good harvests.

Pot for the cult of the Yam Spirit, Ibo village of Osisa, Nigeria.

*Ritual water pot made by Abatan, a
Yoruba potter of Oke-Odan, Nigeria.*

The Yoruba people make a large variety of ritual pots for the worship of many different gods. This one was dedicated to the god Eyinle and was meant to stand on a household altar. Eyinle is a forest deity and a hunter. He also rules over rivers and the sea, and those who worship him must keep in their houses one of these covered pots to hold cool water and water-worn stones.

This vessel was made by a well-known Yoruba artist early in this century. It is closer to sculpture than pottery. The calm, dignified head of the woman on the lid seems to blend into the rounded body of the pot.

Clay sculpture, like pottery, is a very old art in West Africa. Sculptures of baked clay, or terracotta, will last for centuries, even when they are broken and lie buried in the earth. We shall see among clay sculptures some of the oldest art yet found in Africa.

Above left: Side view of water pot.
Above right: The potter Abatan.

Sculpture
of Clay

This terracotta head with its wide open eyes takes us back over two thousand years.

Broken from a whole figure that must have been nearly life-size, the head was dug up by chance in 1954 at Nok, in the center of Nigeria. Before and since that time, many other clay sculptures have been found, probably made by the same people whose settlements were scattered over a wide area of Nigeria.

This so-called Nok Culture seems to have flourished from about 300 B.C. to at least A.D. 200, but little is known about the people of that time. They farmed the land, and they left behind them the relics of furnaces for smelting iron. What gods did they worship? Were their sculptures made for shrines?

Left: Terracotta head. Nok, Nigeria.
Above: Terracotta figure of a chief on his throne. Southern Ghana.

Terracotta group, made in Ibo
village of Osisa, Nigeria, west of
the River Niger. 19th century.

Perhaps the Nok sculptures were for household altars, like the small Ibo group at left, made for the altar of the Yam Spirit. Here we see a man and his two wives with a chicken as a sacrifice to the spirit. Probably the Nok people too offered sacrifices to the deities who protected their fields. Or perhaps the Nok sculptures were for funeral rites, like the heads and clay figures made by the Ashanti.

The figure of a queen mother (above) was modeled for the funeral of a chief in southern Ghana. She belongs to a set of figures that included the chief (page 65), his heir, and some attendants. These sculptures have the same calm dignity as the heads that were made by Ashanti artists, also at the time of death. Neither figures nor heads were put on the grave of the dead person. They were reverently laid in the "place of pots" with food offerings to the ancestors when the funeral rites were over.

Above right: Terracotta head made for funeral rites. Ashanti, Ghana.

Terracotta head made for funeral rites. Lines on neck are a mark of beauty. Ashanti.

68

Nearly a thousand years after the time of the Nok people there was a wonderful flowering of art at Ife in Yorubaland. The sculptures in clay that were made there seem to be related to the art of Nok and probably date back to the dim beginnings of Ife, the first capital of the Yoruba kingdom.

According to the Yoruba people, Ife was the place where the world began. They say that Olorun, the Supreme God, sent his son Obatala down from heaven to create the earth in the midst of the waters. Olorun gave his son a chain, some soil in a snail shell, and a five-toed chicken.

Small clay head, discovered during an excavation in Ife in 1953. Head was part of a larger sculpture; on the cheeks are scars of tribal marks.

On his way Obatala stopped to drink palm wine with some other gods. He drank too much and fell asleep, and that was how Oduduwa, his younger brother, became the maker of the world. Stealing the snail shell and chicken while his brother slept, Oduduwa climbed down from heaven on the chain. He emptied the soil from the shell on the waters, and the chicken busily scratched it and spread it around. Soon the earth was firm enough for Oduduwa to walk on.

When Obatala woke up and found his work done, he was angry and fought with his brother. Then Olorun made peace between them. He appointed Oduduwa to be the first king of Ife, called the *Oni,* and he gave Obatala the task of creating human beings.

Small clay figure of chameleon, dug up by chance in Ife in 1961.

The city of Ife was founded at the place where Oduduwa first
stepped on earth. That spot, surrounded by a grove of trees, is
the holiest shrine in the town, and Ife itself is still a sacred city
and the seat of the Oni. Some of the magnificent sculptures that
we see in the museum near the Oni's palace were discovered by
excavations in the sacred groves and shrines of the town.

Small portrait head from Ife.

The terracotta heads probably represent men and women of the royal court. Most of them look calm and young and beautiful; they have a feeling of peacefulness and strength. Some smaller heads, like the one on page 71, are modeled in a strongly realistic style, and there are lively clay figures of animals. The chameleon reminds us that it was one of these creatures that climbed down the chain with Oduduwa to test the firmness of the new-made earth.

But the artists of Ife were not only sculptors in clay. We have seen how one of them was sent to Benin in the fourteenth century to teach the art of bronze-casting to the people there. By that time the artists of Ife must have had long experience in working with metal, and their most famous works, still surviving today, are cast in bronze.

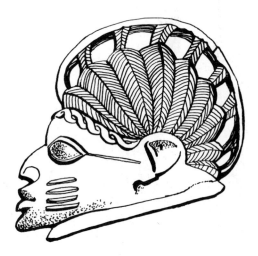

Left: Terracotta head of young woman from Ife, with lines of beauty around her neck (as on Ashanti head, page 68). Above: Gelede mask shows traditional bridal hairdressing, similar to hairstyle of Ife head. Yoruba, Nigeria, early 20th century.

7

Sculpture
of Metal

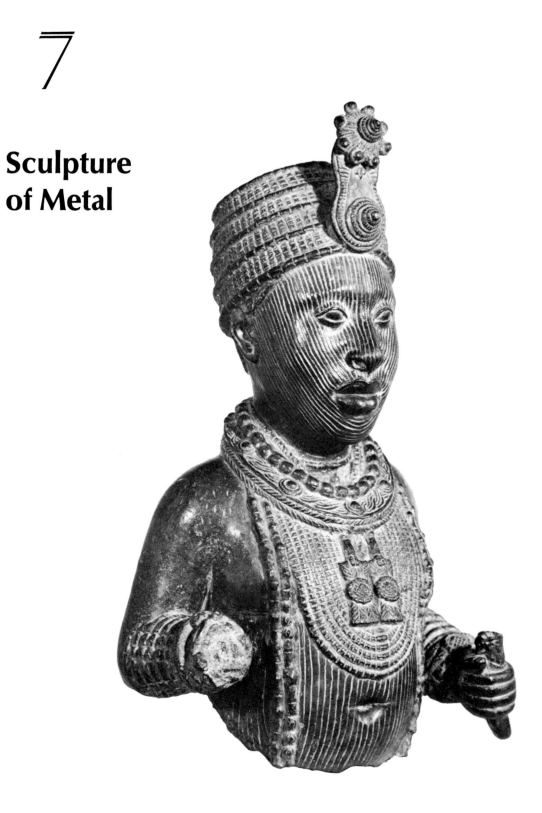

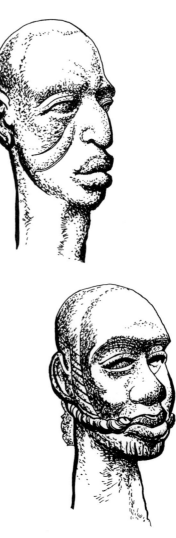

Most of the bronze sculptures of Ife, like those made of clay, were royal portraits.

Here we see the portrait of an Oni, a king of Ife. He wears his crown and many necklaces, and on his chest are the badges of his high office. The lines on his face, and on the faces of many Ife sculptures, are thought to be the scars of tribal marks. Today the custom of tribal marks is dying out, but there are people in northeastern Nigeria who still scar their faces with the long parallel lines that we see here.

Left: Oni, a king of Ife. Bronze.
Above: Small bronze heads from Ife,
forming the tops of a pair of staffs.
The lower one is a prisoner with a
rope gag in his mouth.

75

The seated figure, almost two feet high, is a masterpiece of the Ife bronze-casters, but its present home is far from Ife. For centuries the figure has been kept in the village of Tada on the River Niger, where it is held sacred by the people.

Full-length figures are rare at Ife, and this double portrait of a king and queen is unique. Most of the bronze sculptures are heads, usually life-size. It is thought that they may have been fastened to wooden bodies and used to represent a dead king or queen in the ceremonies after a burial. This idea is supported by an old story that explains why the ancient art of Ife came to a sudden end.

Bronze seated figure. Tada, Nigeria.

Bronze-casting of this statue was so thin the king's face has broken off. Necklaces, queen's skirt, and king's loincloth were originally painted red; queen's crown and hair were painted black.

Bronze head from Ife. Nail hole in neck shows that head was probably attached to a wooden body.

When one of the Onis died, his faithful followers refused to announce his death to the people. Instead they commanded the bronze-casters to make a portrait figure of him, so true to life that everyone would believe the king still lived. The artists did their work well, but their skill was their doom. When the truth came out, the new Oni was filled with rage. He ordered all the artists to be slain, and their art died with them.

Whatever the reason, the art of casting bronze heads seems to have vanished at Ife about six hundred years ago. The fine metalwork of the Yoruba today does not remind us of the sculptures of their ancestors.

Yoruba brass-casting of the present day: ritual staff (left) and rattle.

The true heirs of the traditions of Ife art were the bronze-casters of Benin. They learned the secrets of bronze-casting from Igueghae, the artist of Ife who became their patron, but they were not simply imitators. In the service of the Oba they evolved their own style of art.

Besides making heads of the Obas and queens, and figures of the people at court, the Benin artists developed a new art form—the bronze plaque. In bronze relief sculptures they recorded the Oba's victories in war; the gatherings of chiefs and retainers at the palace; the royal hunts, festivals, and music; and the coming of Portuguese soldiers and traders.

*Bronze figure of hunter, found at
Benin but made by people living
along the lower Niger River.*

Bronze figure of a hornblower, a musician at the court of the Oba of Benin, 16th or 17th century.

While Ife had no contact with white men until the nineteenth century, the Portuguese came to Benin as early as 1486. They kept in close touch with the city. They helped the Oba in some of his military campaigns and supplied his army with guns. Above all, they brought in quantities of metal for the bronze-casters.

The Portuguese may also have brought books and paintings, the first the Edo people had ever seen. These could have inspired the artists of Benin to make the plaques—hundreds of small bronze pictures to be fastened to the wooden pillars of the Oba's vast palace.

This plaque shows a gate of the palace, guarded by soldiers. The snake wriggling down the roof of the turret was actually a huge copper sculpture of a python, one of a number of snakes that adorned the palace roofs.

Ivory box for jewels has carving of two fighting Portuguese in 16th-century dress. Beside them is a scaly anteater.

Bronze plaque showing gate of the Oba's palace.

Bronze plaque of Oba and attendants
by the "Master of the Circled Cross."

The plaque at left shows the Oba himself, supported by two attendants. This was made by a master artist, among the first to work on the plaques. His figures, slim and graceful, stand against a background of engraved crosses in circles, like rich embroidery.

The bronze leopard is a water vessel, used for washing the Oba's hands before religious ceremonies. Metal water jugs shaped like animals were not an African idea, but they were widely used in Europe in the Middle Ages. Perhaps one or two of these vessels came to Benin as trade-goods in the baggage of the Portuguese.

The leopard, strong, fierce, and cunning, was a symbol of kingship in Benin. The Oba even kept his own menagerie of leopards.

The figures of messengers show the close ties between the Edo people of Benin and the Yoruba of Ife. Because the first Oba was a prince of Ife, every succeeding Oba would send a messenger to the Oni of Ife to ask for his support and approval. The signs of the Oni's good will were a staff, a hat, and a cross to be worn as a pendant. The messenger would be rewarded by the gift of a smaller cross to hang around his neck.

Noble bronze cock was made for
an altar of the Oba's "mothers."

Messenger at left dates from mid-16th to mid-17th century; the other was made in the 18th or 19th century.

The messengers and the hornblower (on page 81) were placed on altars in the palace, dedicated to the royal ancestors. Here the reigning Oba made sacrifices to the spirits of his forebears. The well-known Benin heads were also made for these altars of the Oba's "fathers." The later heads were designed to support a huge curved elephant tusk carved with symbolic figures. The high collar, covering the lower part of the face, represents the heavy multiple necklaces of coral beads that are still worn by the Oba for religious ceremonies.

The spirits of the queen mothers were also revered in the palace. This serene and lovely head was made for an altar of the "mothers." Comparing it with the later work of the bronze-casters, we see how their style changed. With a plentiful supply of metal to work with, they made their castings thicker and heavier, and even the heads were overloaded with decoration.

Bronze head of an Oba of Benin, late 16th century.

Left: Head of a queen mother, early
16th century.
Above: Head of an Oba, Late Period.

This small bronze Altar of the Hand belonged to an Oba who reigned in the later part of the eighteenth century. A figure of the ruler, flanked by attendants, stands on the top of the altar. He appears again on the side of it, worked in relief; two raised hands are in the border below. The people of Benin, and others in West Africa, looked on the hand as the symbol of a man's power to be successful in the practical matters of life. Men made sacrifices to the hand to ensure prosperity and good fortune, but when the Oba did this, his sacrifice was not for himself alone. The power of the Oba's hand affected the fortunes of his whole kingdom.

Altar of the Hand.

By the time this altar was made the Obas were no longer strong warrior-kings, leading their armies out to extend the boundaries of the empire. The Benin empire was beginning to fall apart, although it would not be destroyed until the capital city was captured by the British in 1897.

While the old empire of Benin was declining, torn apart by civil wars between rival chiefs, the Fon kingdom of Dahomey, far away to the west, was at the height of its power.

The kings of Dahomey, whose history was recorded in the storytelling cloths of bright appliqué (page 22), kept a whole army of craftsmen at work in the palace at Abomey. Skilled smiths made the symbols of the king's authority—the ceremonial scepters with their sculptured heads of silver or iron. The scepter was carried in the king's hand or hooked over his left shoulder as he sat enthroned. His messengers would bear the scepters to the ends of the kingdom to show that the words they spoke were truly the words of the king. Wherever the royal scepter was seen, the king's power was feared and respected.

Ceremonial scepter made of wood and iron. Fon, Dahomey.

The metalworkers of Dahomey also made hundreds of little brass figures, not as religious offerings but simply to decorate the palace, to display the king's wealth, and surely to give him delight. The little figures provided a panorama in miniature of the life of the kingdom.

Here we see a royal procession. The king goes forth from his palace, carried in a litter like a low-slung hammock. He sits at his ease, smoking a long pipe, while his retainers fan him and carry the ceremonial umbrellas. The king is followed by his musicians, for no procession was complete without music. One of the drums is so large it is carried on a man's head with the drummer plying his drumsticks from behind. We can almost hear the beat of the drums and the ringing note of the iron gongs.

The figure of the old man might well be a spectator, watching the procession pass by through the dusty streets of Abomey. He is a typical African elder, a man with the wisdom of many years. All younger men must honor him and listen to his words.

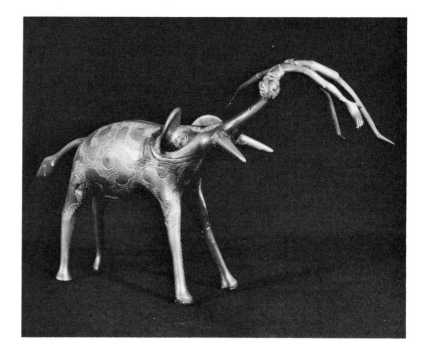

94

Hunting scenes inspired the makers of the figures at left. A man is tossed in the air by a wild elephant, while a successful hunter returns home with his flintlock gun, his dog at his heels, and the kill—a small antelope—slung from his shoulder.

The figure of a woman kneeling in prayer is filled with the strong faith of the Fon people. They worship many of the same gods as their neighbors, the Yoruba, and all through their lives there are ceremonies, sacrifices, and religious festivals.

Tiny brass figures are made today in Dahomey, though not as a royal art, and the kind of people they show can still be met in towns and villages. Local rulers sit enthroned, scepter in hand; people drum and dance; farmers hoe the fields; and craftsmen, like the blacksmith, make the things the people need.

Brass figures. Fon.

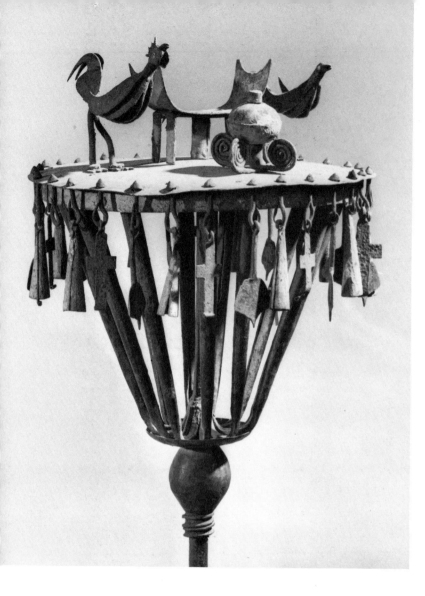

The blacksmiths of Dahomey rank with weavers as the most respected craftsmen in the land. Their craft is passed down in families and they worship Gu, the god of iron. Many smiths simply hammer out hoes, axe-heads, and machetes for farmers. Others have the skill to make the elaborate wrought-iron staffs that are set up in the shrines of the ancestors, and some make the iron double gongs that add their bell-like notes to the rhythm of the drum orchestra.

Wrought-iron top of staff for ancestral shrine. Fon.

A village blacksmith in Dahomey.

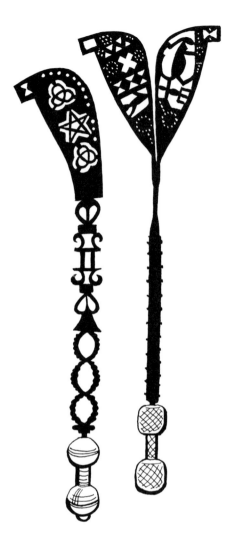

As the scepter is the symbol of kingship in Dahomey, in the Ashanti kingdom it is the state sword, with its decorated iron blade and gilded hilt.

When an Ashanti ruler sits in state, the swords are held before him by his sword-bearers. Lesser chiefs will swear allegiance to the ruler on these swords, which are also carried by royal messengers.

Fine metalwork is important too among the furnishings of an Ashanti palace. Beautiful brass vessels known as *kuduo* are designed to hold offerings at religious ceremonies and also to serve as containers for gold dust, precious beads, and jewelry.

A kuduo is made by the same lost-wax method as the gold-weights, and its lid may be crowned with little figures of animals or people.

When we look at other palace furniture, especially the stools that are so necessary to the Ashanti, we must turn to the work of carvers in wood and ivory.

Above: State swords of wood and iron.
Above right: Brass goldweight in
the shape of a chameleon. All Ashanti.

Covered brass vessel (kuduo).

The Art
of the Carver:
Furnishing
the Palace

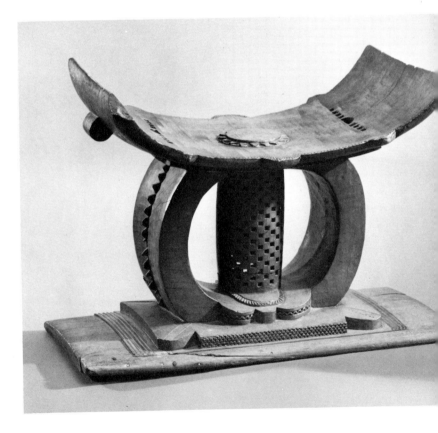

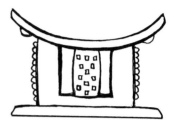

The Ashanti people say: "There are no secrets between a man and his stool."

For them, the stool is far more than just a seat. It is the first present from a father to his small child, and the child soon learns that a stool contains the soul of its owner. When he is not sitting on the stool, it must be tilted on its side so that no evil spirit may sit there.

Making stools, then, is an important task of the Ashanti woodcarver. Before he sets to work, the carver will offer a prayer to the spirit of the tree that gave the wood, and to his tools—his adze, knives, and chisels.

He carves the stool from a single piece of wood. The variety of design comes in the decoration of the legs or the column between the flat base and the curved seat. The carver knows that the designs have meanings and that some of them can only be used on certain stools. There are men's stools, women's stools, and those designed for kings, queens, or priests.

Left: Chief's stool. Ashanti, Ghana.
Above (top to bottom): Woman's stool,
usually a gift from husband to wife;
"Moon stool," used by men and women;
"Cross-shaped stool," used by the
Asantehene.

As the dwelling-place of his soul, a chief's stool is a symbol of his power and of the unity of his people. The stool he uses as a throne may be plated with silver or gold, but when he dies it is blackened all over with smoke. Then it is placed in the "stool house" with the Black Stools of his ancestors. The chief's soul, and the souls of his forebears, live on in the Black Stools, and offerings of food and drink are placed on the stools when prayers are addressed to the ancestors.

The Golden Stool of the Ashanti contains the soul of all the people. Said to be made of solid gold, the Stool came down from heaven to the first great king of the Ashanti, Osei Tutu, three hundred years ago. We have seen how the Ashanti made war against King Adinkra, who dared to make a copy of the Golden Stool. The Asantehene displays the Stool only at the most important festivals and ceremonies. Then it lies on its own throne, a high-backed chair plated with silver.

Queen mother's stool plated with silver. Ashanti.

Decorated chairs are often used as thrones by Ashanti rulers, and there are different designs of chairs for joyful or solemn occasions.

Whenever a ruler sits in state or goes forth in procession, one man stands out among the officials who accompany him. This is the linguist, the chief's spokesman, known by his carved staff of office (see page 38). The linguist is one of the principal men in the state, for it is he who relays the chief's words to the people and gives back their answers to the chief. He must be a wise man, knowing the laws and customs and the ancient wisdom of the proverbs. The carving on the top of his staff usually illustrates a proverb, and as the linguist addresses the people, his staff speaks its own silent message.

The carving of the hand and egg warns the ruler that governing a state is like holding an egg, a tricky and delicate task. Squeeze too hard and the egg will break; hold it too loosely and it will fall and smash.

A head with three faces shows that wise counsel should come from several men, not just one, while the pineapple, which must not be picked until it is ripe, suggests the need for long thought before making decisions. The Ashanti are never in a hurry to make up their minds. "If no time is allowed for cooking," they say, "you eat uncooked food."

Above left: Chief's chair, decorated with brass nails.
Above: Linguists' staffs, gilded wood.

103

Ashanti ruler in procession, borne
on a litter and followed by players
of royal drums.

The top of the big silken umbrella that shelters the chief from the sun also carries a carving. It may be a bird or a man, a hand holding a sword, or even a cooking pot on the hearthstones.

A fly whisk made from a long horsetail is usually in the chief's hand when he sits in state, and the wooden handles of fly whisks give the carvers another chance to show their skill. Among the Agni and Baule people of the Ivory Coast—neighbors of the Ashanti—the handles of fly whisks are beautifully carved with figures of animals and birds. Baule artists frequently cover the finished carvings with thinly beaten gold and engrave the gold with a network of geometric patterns.

Wooden handles for fly whisks with elephants carved on top. Baule, Ivory Coast.

Wooden handle of a fly whisk.
Agni, Ivory Coast.

106

In the hands of a Baule carver the wooden beater for an iron gong takes the form of a small standing figure, as elegant and smoothly finished as the larger Baule sculptures (page 121). Musicians, as we have seen, were essential members of the household of a chief or a king, and their instruments were often masterpieces of the carver's art.

Above left: Wooden gong beater. Baule, Ivory Coast.
Above: Ceremonial scepter of wood and silver. Fon, Dahomey.

107

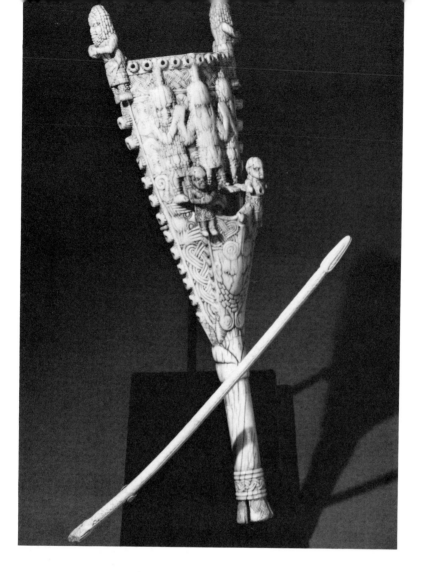

An ivory carver of Benin, in the sixteenth century, made this magnificent double gong, with its relief carving of the Oba and his attendants. The Oba himself would have carried and played this gong during public ceremonies in Benin.

The drum from Guinea and the tall pedestal on which it stands have been made into a strong unified design. Here, the fine carving of a woman supports the drum on her head. Sculptured figures on a larger scale can be used as pillars, or house-posts, to support the roofs of buildings. Some of the best-known Yoruba sculptors have made house-posts for the palaces of their kings.

Ivory gong and striker. Benin, Nigeria.

Left: Ceremonial drum can be lifted off top of stand, above frieze of heads. Southern Baga, Guinea. Above: Ivory cup supported by figures of four men. Benin, Nigeria.

One of these artists was a man named Arowogun, who died in 1954. He carved this house-post in the shape of a mounted warrior, a favorite subject of Yoruba sculptors.

The palace doors are also Arowogun's work. Each of the little scenes is a vivid picture of life in Yorubaland when Nigeria was still a British colony. There are Yoruba hunters with their guns; drummers and dancers; women with babies on their backs and women pounding grain; armed men on horseback and others bustling about on bicycles; and the busy officials of the colonial government.

Housepost carved by Arowogun.

Wooden palace doors by Olowe of Ise.

Another great Yoruba sculptor was Olowe of Ise. In the early years of this century he was famous for making doors and house-posts in his own distinctive style. The figures in his relief carvings stand out from their background like sculptures in the round.

This pair of doors, made for the palace at Ikere-Ekiti in eastern Yorubaland, commemorates the day in 1895 when the British district officer came to visit the *Ogoga*, the ruler of Ekiti. The white man, shown as a rather comical little person, rides in a large litter while a train of shackled prisoners carries his baggage. The dignified Yoruba king waits to receive him, seated on a throne and wearing a beaded crown, with his wives and elders in attendance.

These handsome doors added splendor to the king's palace. They also recorded an important day in the history of the king-dom and told all men of the Ogoga's wealth and power.

Bandele, a Yoruba woodcarver, at work.

In palace furnishings, we see art in the service of men. Yet most of the work of the carvers in Yorubaland, and throughout West Africa, was in the service of gods and spirits. The spirit-world was very close to the people. For them, the Supreme God, the gods of earth and waters, and the spirits of ancestors were invisible but always present. Prayers and offerings and holy festivals were a part of daily living.

Customs and ways of prayer and worship were different among different groups of people; but everywhere the carvers of wood and ivory, the makers of images and masks, used their greatest skill to create works that would be pleasing to the deities.

The artists served as a link between men and the unseen world, and among the Ashanti they were called the linguists, or spokesmen, of the Supreme God, Creator of the Universe.

Wooden mask. Ibibio, Nigeria.

Left: Figure used in ceremonies of
a secret society. Mende, Sierra Leone.
Above: Bowl for palm nuts used in
divination. Fon, Dahomey.

9

The Art
of the Carver:
Gods, Spirits,
and Ancestors

For the Fon people and the Yoruba there are more than four hundred gods. Most people have one particular god to whom they give special devotion. Among the Yoruba it may be Shango, the god of thunder; Obatala, the creator of men; Eyinle, the god of forests and waters; or Ogun, who is the patron of those who work with iron, including the drivers of cars and trucks.

But there is one god to whom all people may turn for guidance in their daily lives. He is the god of divination, called Ifa by the Yoruba people and Fa by the Fon. Ifa's spokesmen are the diviners, and to do their work they use wooden trays, cups, and "tappers," which are beautifully made by the woodcarvers of Yorubaland and Dahomey.

Left: Bowl to hold nuts for divination. Fon, Dahomey.
Above: Yoruba diviner at work, with tray and covered bowl for palm nuts.

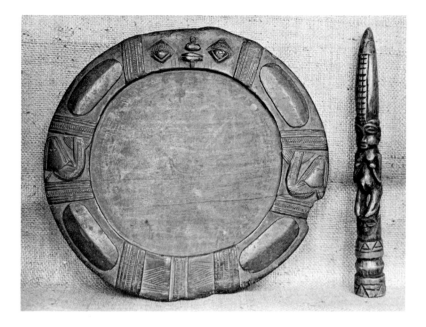

When a person comes to him for advice, the diviner spreads sand or wood dust on the tray. The designs around the edge of the tray always include the face of Eshu, the messenger of the gods. The tray above has carvings of mudfish, the symbol of Olokun, the god of wealth, and oval-shaped thunderbolts of Shango.

To attract the attention of Ifa, the diviner raps on the board with his tapper, which often has a little rattle inside it. Then he takes sixteen palm nuts from his bowl and tosses them swiftly from right hand to left. If two nuts remain in the right hand, he makes one line with his finger on the sanded tray. For one nut, he makes two lines.

After he has thrown the nuts and marked the tray four times, he studies the pattern of marks and speaks the long poem that is linked with that particular pattern. He knows scores of these poems by heart, and he often tells a story to help explain the meaning of the verses to the person who has come to him.

Divining tray with wooden tapper
carved in shape of a kneeling woman.
Yoruba, Nigeria.

People come with problems in their families or their work. If a Yoruba mother gives birth to twins, she consults a diviner at once. Twins are special children, protected by Shango. The diviner may tell the mother to have a pair of wooden figures made, representing the twins. He is almost certain to advise this if one or both of the twins should die. The mother dresses the two small *ibeji* in beads, bracelets, and cowrie shells. She wraps them up warmly, carries them about like babies, and even dances with them in her arms.

*Above left: Pair of tappers for divination. Fon, Dahomey.
Above: Ibeji figure, representing a girl twin. Yoruba.*

119

Above: Akua-ba doll. *Ashanti, Ghana.*
Right: Small wooden figure. Ibo,
Nigeria.

The *akua-ba* dolls made by the Ashanti also represent babies. They are carried by little girls and by women who are expecting a child. The women believe that a new baby will be beautiful, with a round face and high, smooth forehead, if the mother keeps one of these fertility dolls.

Many West African peoples make wooden figures as dwelling-places for the spirits of the dead, who watch over the fortunes of their descendants and listen to their prayers. These "ancestor figures" are not intended to be portraits. They are never made to look old and wrinkled. An ancestor should be shown as someone strong, quiet, thoughtful, and wise, a person of coolness and dignity. Different peoples have expressed this idea in their own distinctive ways.

Finely finished figure is typical of work of Baule artists in Ivory Coast.

121

The peoples of southeastern Nigeria, living in scattered forest villages or among the waterways of the Niger Delta, developed some of the most varied styles of sculpture.

These three figures from the delta region break the rule that an African sculpture is always carved from a single block of wood. The figures sit against a screen made of many small pieces of cane, and their bodies, legs, and arms have been carved separately and fitted together. The group was made in the nineteenth century, in memory of a man of the Ijo people who had become wealthy through trade with the white men.

The old delta town of Brass, named after its principal import, was a busy center of trade in those days. The majestic statue known as the Lady of Brass is supposed to have come from there. The figure probably represents a member of an Ijo merchant family. The carver might have been influenced in his work by seeing the carved figureheads of sailing vessels that came to the port of Brass from Europe and America.

Left: Funerary screen, wood and cane. Ijo, Nigeria.
Above: "Lady of Brass," probably made by an Ijo artist in 19th century.

Another sculpture by an Ijo artist is quite different in form and purpose. The *ejiri* figure is a personal shrine, believed to give power to the man who keeps it in his house. The head of the household is shown mounted on a strange elephant-like creature that stands for the guardian spirit of the house.

The *ikenga* carving is a Shrine of the Hand, like the ornate bronze altar made for the Oba of Benin (page 90). Sacrifices to the hand gave a man power to achieve success whether he was a village farmer growing yams or a king commanding an empire.

These personal sculptures, and many of the ancestor figures too, were never meant to be seen by outsiders. They were hidden away in dark and secret places. Most sculptures that are seen in public only come out at certain times of year, at the festivals and ceremonies for which they were made. Then they will often appear against a background of music and the swirling movement and rhythm of the dance.

Above: Ikenga *shrine. Ibo, Nigeria.*
Right: Ejiri *figure. Ijo, Nigeria.*

The Yoruba sculptures known as "dance wands" are designed to be carried in dances for the gods. Here we see three stages in the making of a new dance wand for the shrine of Shango. The carver has chosen a log of wood to work on and cuts into it with swift sure strokes of his adze. He carries the design in his head, and soon the shapes he has in mind begin to appear in the wood.

The main figure on the dance wand is to be a priest of Shango. On one side of him there will be a crouching woman, a worshiper of Shango's wife, Oya. On the other side the carver makes a drummer, playing one of Shango's *bata* drums, and at the top he carves a ram and a dog, animals sacred to the thunder god.

Two stages in carving of a dance wand
by Duga, the Yoruba artist who is
shown at work on page 11.

126

When the figures are fully formed, he takes a smaller adze for the finer carving. He finishes the details and the smoothing with a knife. Lastly he paints the figures in black, red, tan, and light blue. His brush is a stick with a soft chewed end, and the colors are made from wood and white chalk, ground-up stone, and the leaves of the indigo plant.

The finished dance wand will be stored in the shrine of Shango until it is needed for the festival in honor of the god. Then the carving will be grasped in the hand of a dancer who is clothed in a coat of cowrie shells. The bata drums will play and the dancer will become possessed by the strong spirit of the god of thunder.

Above left: Painting the finished wand.
Above: A dance wand with figure of
a worshiper of Ifa. Yoruba, Nigeria.

Much larger sculptures are also carried in Yoruba dances. This horseman is carved on top of an Epa mask. The god Epa was a woodcarver himself, and the masks for his festival are masterpieces of the carver's art, sometimes weighing as much as sixty pounds and crowned by whole groups of figures.

In the Epa dance, performed in certain Yoruba villages every two years, the masks go leaping through the air, mounted on the heads of strong young dancers, to bring prosperity and well-being to the people.

Above: Epa wood mask. Yoruba, Nigeria.
Above right: Wood mask. Dan, Ivory Coast.

West African masks, in all their many forms, are made for movement, music, and the dance. Masks may be male or female, but the dancers who wear them are almost always men. There are masks of ancestors and of the spirits of rivers, forests, and fields; masks of secret societies and initiations; masks that bring fertility or keep order or simply make people laugh. All have special reasons for their making and special times to appear before the people who are allowed to see them.

Above left: Headpiece representing a violent and ugly spirit. Ibo, Nigeria. Above: Helmet mask worn by women leaders of Bundu society. Mende, Sierra Leone.

*Above: Horned headpiece, face covered
with animal skin. Ekoi, Nigeria.
Right: Antelope mask. Guro, Ivory Coast.*

But masks are not just to be looked at. They must be heard and felt and waited for in breathless expectation, often in the darkness of the night or under the cold light of the moon, when the air is filled with the pounding of drums.

This is how it is in a little village in Yoruba-land on the night of the Gelede festival, the night to worship the Earth Mother and control the powers of evil.

Top: Water-spirit mask, worn on top of head and used in dance dramas in the Niger Delta region. Ijo, Nigeria. Above: Old mask representing ancestral spirit. Ibibio, Nigeria.

Darkness has fallen and the drums have called the people together around the open dancing-place. An archway of palm branches has been set up as an entrance for the masks to come through. Men are already dancing on the bare beaten earth when the first masks appear.

Below the pale painted faces of the Gelede masks the bright-colored costumes cover the dancers from head to foot, flapping and swinging as they dance and sing. One of the masks is the wife of Efe, the great and powerful one whom everybody is waiting for. She dances to the drums with a fly whisk swishing to and fro in one hand and iron leg rattles clanking to the rhythm of her swiftly moving feet.

She calls to Efe to come forth. Everyone watches the palm-frond gateway and the darkness beyond it. The dancing and drumming quicken in the arena, and there is a second call to Efe. Again the drums play, and then a gong sounds for silence. At the third call the thin notes of a flute are heard in the darkness and then the voice of Efe singing. The singers in the dancing-place take up the song, and at last the huge white Efe mask comes out of the darkness behind the palm-leaf gate—a mighty figure with many-colored draperies swaying around him. A gun is fired with a deafening blast, and Efe comes stamping into the open to greet and to pay homage to the priestess of the great Earth Mother.

Gelede mask. Yoruba, Dahomey.

Then, all through the night, Efe will dance and sing and tell stories to celebrate this festival in which everyone has a part—as spectator, dancer, drummer, or singer, as carver of masks or maker of costumes. Tonight all the arts are woven together in the lives of the people, not only to bring joy and excitement and suspense but to secure the blessings of the Great Mother and the safety of the village from the powers of witchcraft.

In the bright moonlight and under the heavy shadow of the trees, as the bare feet pound on the bare earth and the tall white mask moves in splendor, the people and their arts and their faith are united with the land that feeds them and gives them life, the land of their ancestors.

Great Efe mask in Gelede dance.

133

Artists of
the New Age

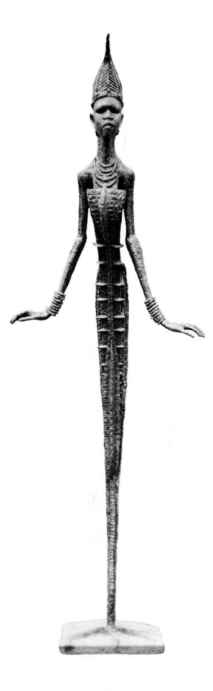

After the night of the Gelede dance we are back in the heart of a city. The traffic roars down the street and rivers of people stream along the pavements. They sweep us along past the bright shop fronts and the fruit-sellers' stalls and the hawkers of watches and ball-point pens and ink-stained secondhand books. The latest popular music blares from the record shops, and people crowd to listen. The drums beat now for the high life and catch new rhythms from across the Atlantic. What do these people care for old woodcarvings, old music, and all the arts that were once a part of life?

Many people have come here from villages, far away along dusty roads. They have left behind forever the old rhythms of planting time and harvest, festivals and days of worship. They are reaching out for new and better ways of living. Where is the place for the African artist in this new kind of world?

People who are sad about the passing of old African arts, and the fact that there are fewer artists and craftsmen working in traditional ways, forget that art is always changing. An art that does not change becomes as dry and dead as modern copies of old African masks.

Left: Sculptured cement screen by Adebisi Akanji at Oshogbo, Nigeria. Above: Bronze sculpture, "The Awakening," by Ben Enwonwu, outside Nigerian Museum, Lagos.

135

We cannot see what African wood sculpture was like five hundred or a thousand years ago, for wood in the tropics is too quickly destroyed by rot and termites. But the enduring arts of Nok, Ife, and Benin, modeled in clay and cast in metal, show how African art has changed through the centuries.

Africa has never been completely cut off from the outside world, and within the continent the movements of African peoples have helped in the exchange and spread of new ideas in art. Even a few traders, invaders, or people on the move can carry with them ideas that artists are quick to borrow and to use —a new form of carving, a different kind of dance, or a musical instrument never heard before.

The arrival of white men in West Africa led to a shattering invasion of new ideas. In the colonial time it was not only the ancient African kingdoms that were conquered by the invading armies of Western nations. Old beliefs were destroyed, and there was a breaking-up of the well-ordered world in which the artist had his place.

When the African nations gained their freedom, there was a new freedom for artists too. Those who had had a Western education were already freed from working in the traditional ways of the village artists and craftsmen. Some of them had been imitating the styles and subjects of Western art. Now these artists turned to the art of their own people, which they had been taught to look down on. At last they could express themselves as Africans.

The powerful sculptures of Vincent Kofi of Ghana show how this can be done. Kofi has had training in England and America, but his work grows from his own land. It takes courage for a West African sculptor to carve in wood, as this artist does, without being overwhelmed by the famous works of the ancient sculptors. Vincent Kofi carves with a feeling for the wood, almost with the reverence of the old woodcarvers, who used to sacrifice to the tree before cutting it to make a sculpture or a drum.

Wood sculpture, "Pregnant Mother and Child," by Vincent Kofi. Ghana.

Some sculptors, turning away from woodcarving, work on old themes using new techniques. A Yoruba artist, Adebisi Akanji, has taken the theme of scenes from Yoruba life, which we have seen carved on the doors of palaces. But this artist has used cement as his medium, and instead of adorning a palace his open-work screen decorates a service station in the town of Oshogbo and brings art into the street for everyone to see (page 134).

Across from the service station is the Mbari Mbayo Club, which has made Oshogbo a lively center of art. Many young artists, often self-taught, have worked there, making oil paintings, ink drawings, and block prints, resist-dyed hangings and even pictures in beadwork. Although they may use materials from the

Wood panel by Osagie Osifo of the
Crucifixion, at the Catholic Chapel,
University of Ibadan, Nigeria.

West, their subjects are drawn from the life they know and from the stories and deep beliefs that belong to their Yoruba inheritance. We find prints of drummers and dancers, a village festival, a vision of Shango, or of Obatala at the work of creation.

Woodblock print, "Creation," by Tijani Mayakiri. Ife, Nigeria.

Craftsmen too have joined in the awakening of the arts, and sometimes, in a spirit of experiment, ancient rules have been broken. Young men in Dahomey have taken up the woman's craft of pottery, and some of their pots have blossomed into ceramic sculpture.

This is an exciting time for African art, but for the new artists the way is not clear or easy. They have left behind the small world of the village where all the arts are bound together as a part of life. Their work is not needed by their people in the same way that wood sculptures and masks were needed. The background of a contemporary sculpture is a public building on a busy street, not a village dancing-place. But that does not make the sculpture less African.

The artists of West Africa today are shaping an art that will be neither an imitation of the West nor a dead copy of the African past. Their work is their own creation. Their horizon is as wide as the great sky over forest and grassland and city, but their feet are firmly planted on the red soil of their ancient land.

Through their art they can speak with a clear voice, not only to their own people but to the world.

Bronze sculpture, "Awakening Africa," by Vincent Kofi. Ghana.

List of Illustrations

Bold number indicates book page

17 Resist-dyed cloth (*adire eleko*). Cotton dyed with indigo. Yoruba, Nigeria. 74¼″ x 65″. UCLA Museum of Cultural History. Catalog no. X66-1149. Photo: Larry Dupont.

18 Man's loom, Dahomey. Photo: United Nations.

19 (Top) Yoruba woman's loom at Ado-Ekiti, Nigeria. Photo: Frank Willett.
(Bottom) Woman's loom, Nigeria. Photo: Federation of Nigeria, Information Service.

20 Men's dress. Yoruba, Nigeria.

21 Royal costume. Fon, Dahomey. Length of tunic: 35″. The Brooklyn Museum.

22 Appliqué cloth. Fon, Dahomey. Collected at Abomey, Dahomey, July 1969. University of Denver, Anthropology Department Collection (No. 5628). Photo: Marilane McCarthy.

23 Man sewing appliqué at Abomey, Dahomey. Photo: United Nations.

24 Symbols from appliqué cloth. Fon, Dahomey.

25 Men's dress. Ashanti, Ghana.

26 Kente cloth. Cotton and silk. Ashanti, Ghana. 84″ x 51″. Courtesy Museum of Primitive Art.

27 Strip of kente cloth. Cotton and silk. Ashanti, Ghana. Collection C. Price. Photo: Sandi Olivo.

28 Adinkra stamps. Carved from pieces of calabash, wood handle. Height (l. to r.): 3⅛″; 2⅛″. Collection C. Price. Photo: Sandi Olivo.

29 Printing adinkra cloth, Ghana. Photo: C. Price.

30 Adinkra cloth. Cotton with stamped design. Ashanti, Ghana. Collection Jeannette Mirsky. Photo: Sandi Olivo.

31 Designs of adinkra stamps. Ashanti, Ghana.

32 Two girdle masks. Bronze. Benin, Nigeria, 18th century. Height (l. to r.): 6½″; 6¾″. University Museum, University of Pennsylvania.

33 Pendant mask. Gold. Baule, Ivory Coast. Height: 3½″. Courtesy Museum of Primitive Art.

34 (Top) Scales for weighing gold dust. Brass. Ashanti, Ghana. University Museum, University of Pennsylvania.
(Bottom) Goldweight. Brass. Ashanti, Ghana.

35 (Top) Three goldweights: birds on a tree; a chief on his stool; two crocodiles with one stomach. Brass. Ashanti, Ghana.
(Bottom) Goldweights and box for gold dust. Brass. Ashanti, Ghana. University Museum, University of Pennsylvania.

36 Box for gold dust. Brass. Ashanti, Ghana. Length: 3½″. Courtesy Museum of Primitive Art.

37 Necklace. Gold. Ashanti, Ghana. Length: 15½″. Courtesy Museum of Primitive Art.

38 Ruler with his family and retainers, Ghana. Photo: United Nations.

39 Brass-caster making wax model. Benin, Nigeria. Photo: Philip Dark.

40 (Top) Brass-caster pouring metal into mold. Benin, Nigeria.
(Bottom left) Ornamental hip mask. Brass. Benin, Nigeria, 1959. Both photos: Philip Dark.
(Bottom right) Girdle mask. Bronze. Benin, Nigeria, about 1850. Height: 7″. University Museum, University of Pennsylvania.

41 Double armlet. Ivory inlaid with bronze. Benin, Nigeria, probably before 1550. Height: 5¼″. The British Museum.

42 Pectoral or waist mask. Ivory. Benin, Nigeria, early 16th century. Height: 9¾″. The British Museum.

43 (Top) Double armlet. Ivory. Yoruba, Nigeria. Height: 6¾″. The British Museum.
(Bottom) Leopard. Ivory with inlaid metal spots. Benin, Nigeria. Length: 11″. The British Museum.

44 Beaded royal crown. Yoruba, Nigeria, late 19th or early 20th century. Height: 36½″. The Brooklyn Museum, Caroline A. L. Pratt Fund and others.

45 Drummer and players of *shekere* (calabash rattles). Yoruba, Nigeria.

46 Musician of Brikama, Gambia, with *kora*. Photo: Marc Pevar.

47 Calabash drum and xylophone. Ghana.

48 (Left) Tools of Isola, Yoruba calabash carver of Babaloke, Nigeria. Tools now in Manchester Museum, England.
(Right) Isola beginning to carve a calabash. Both photos: Frank Willett.

49 Later stage of Isola's carving. Photo: Frank Willett.

50 (Top) Carved calabash. Yoruba, Nigeria, about 1870. Diameter: 10⅝″. Collection C. Price. Photo: Aldo Merusi.
(Bottom) Calabash for dyeing fingernails with henna. Yoruba, Ilorin, Nigeria. Height: 12¼″. UCLA Museum of Cultural History, Gift of the Wellcome Trust. Catalog no. X65-9052. Photo: Larry Dupont.

51 Isola, Yoruba calabash carver of Babaloke, Nigeria. Photo: Frank Willett.

52 Carved calabash. Fon, Dahomey. Diameter: 8″. The Herskovits Collection. Photo: Frank Willett.

53 Carved calabash. Fon, Dahomey. Diameter: 8¼″. Collection C. Price. Photo: Aldo Merusi.

54 Potter at Use, near Benin, Nigeria. Photo: Frank Willett.

55 Water pot in the shape of an animal. Eastern Ghana. Ghana National Museum, Accra.

56 Pot with molded ornament. Ibo, Nigeria. Height: 17½″. The British Museum.

57 (Top) Potter at Use, Nigeria.
(Bottom) Pot with incised decoration, made by the potter of Use. Both photos: Frank Willett.

58 (Right) Red pottery vessel from Man, Ivory Coast. Height: 4½″. Collection C. Price. Photo: Sandi Olivo.
(Left) Family pot (*Abusua Kuruwa*). Ashanti, Ghana. Ghana National Museum, Accra.

59 Potter shaping large water vessel, Dahomey. Photo: United Nations/ILO.

60 "Jawbone pot." Ashanti, Ghana. Height: 18″. The British Museum.

61 Pot for cult of the Yam Spirit. Ibo village of Osisa, west of the lower Niger, Nigeria, 19th century. Height of complete pot: 19″. The British Museum. Detail of sculptured decoration ⌐(top); complete pot (bottom).

62 Front view of pot for the cult of Eyinle, made by Abatan, a Yoruba potter of Oke-Odan, Nigeria. The Smithsonian Institution.

63 (Left) Side view of pot on page 62. The Smithsonian Institution.
(Right) The potter Abatan. Photo: Robert F. Thompson.

64 Head. Terracotta. Nok, Nigeria, 1st or 2nd century B.C. Height: 14″. The Nigerian Museum, Lagos. Photo: Frank Willett.

65 Funerary figure of a chief. Terracotta. Southern Ghana. Ghana National Museum, Accra.

66 Group for cult of the Yam Spirit. Terracotta. Ibo village of Osisa, Nigeria, 19th century. Height: 18½″. The British Museum.

67 (Left) Funerary figure of a queen mother. Terracotta. Southern Ghana. Ghana National Museum, Accra.

(Right) Funerary head. Terracotta. Ashanti, Ghana. Height: 12⅜″. Courtesy Museum of Primitive Art.

68 Funerary head. Terracotta. Ashanti, Ghana (Twifo style). Height: 8″. Courtesy Museum of Primitive Art.

69 Head. Terracotta. Ife, Nigeria. Height: 5″. Ife Museum. Photo: Frank Willett.

70 Chameleon. Terracotta. Ife, Nigeria. Height: 4¼″. Ife Museum. Photo: Frank Willett.

71 Head. Terracotta. Ife, Nigeria. Height: 3¼″. Ife Museum. Photo: Frank Willett.

72 Head. Terracotta. Ife, Nigeria. Height: 9⅝″. Ife Museum. Photo: Francis Speed and Frank Willett.

73 Gelede mask. Wood and paint. Yoruba, Nigeria. Height: 9½″. UCLA Museum of Cultural History, Gift of the Wellcome Trust.

74 Oni, or king, of Ife (upper part of a standing figure). Bronze. Ife, Nigeria. Height: 14⁹⁄₁₆″. Ife Museum. Photo: Frank Willett.

75 Heads of two bronze staffs. Ife, Nigeria. Heights: 3¼″. Ife Museum.

76 Seated figure. Bronze. Village of Tada on the River Niger, Nigeria. Height: 21″. Photo: Frank Willett.

77 Oni and queen of Ife. Bronze. Ife, Nigeria. Height: 11¼″. Ife Museum. Photo: Frank Willett.

78 Head. Bronze. Ife, Nigeria. Height: 12″. Ife Museum. Photo: Frank Willett.

79 (Left) *Edan*, or ritual staff, made for the Ogboni society. Brass. Yoruba, Nigeria. Height: 15″. The British Museum.
(Right) Rattle, made for the Ogboni society. Brass. Yoruba, Nigeria. Height: 14½″. The British Museum.

80 Huntsman. Bronze. "Lower Niger Bronze Industry," Nigeria. Height: 14½″. The British Museum.

81 Hornblower. Bronze. Benin, Nigeria, 1550–1650. Height: 24½″. The British Museum.

82 Box. Ivory. Benin, Nigeria, probably 1550–1650. Length: 6½″. University Museum, University of Pennsylvania.

83 Plaque showing gate of the Oba's palace. Bronze. Benin, Nigeria. Height: 22½″. The British Museum.

84 Plaque showing the Oba and attendants, by the "Master of the Circled Cross." Bronze. Benin, Nigeria, late 16th century. Height: 16½". The British Museum.

85 Water vessel in the shape of a leopard. Bronze. Benin, Nigeria, 1550–1650. Height: 12¼". The British Museum.

86 Cock. Bronze. Benin, Nigeria, about 1750. Height: 20". The British Museum.

87 Two messengers. Bronze. Benin, Nigeria, 1550–1650 (left) and 18th century (right). Height (l. to r.): 25½"; 22½". The British Museum.

88 Head of an Oba. Bronze. Benin, Nigeria, late 16th century. Height: 9¼". The British Museum.

89 (Left) Head of a queen mother. Bronze. Benin, Nigeria, early 16th century. Height: 15½". The British Museum.
(Right) Head of an Oba. Bronze. Benin, Nigeria, 18th or 19th century. Height: 20½". The British Museum.

90 Altar of the Hand. Bronze. Benin, Nigeria, 18th century. Height: 18". The British Museum.

91 Ceremonial staff. Wood and iron. Fon, Dahomey. Height: 19½". Courtesy Museum of Primitive Art.

92-93 King and retainers (side view of group on page 8). Brass. Fon, Dahomey. Courtesy American Museum of Natural History.

93 Old man. Brass. Fon, Dahomey. Courtesy American Museum of Natural History.

94 (Top) Hunter and dog. Brass. Fon, Dahomey. Height: 7¾". The Herskovits Collection.
(Bottom) Man and elephant. Brass. Fon, Dahomey. Height: 6". The Herskovits Collection. Both photos: Frank Willett.

95 Woman in prayer. Brass. Fon, Dahomey. Courtesy American Museum of Natural History.

96 Staff for ancestral shrine. Iron, wood, and paint. Fon, Dahomey. Height: 56⅛". Courtesy Museum of Primitive Art.

97 Village blacksmith, Dahomey. Photo: United Nations.

98 (Left) State swords. Wood and iron. Ashanti, Ghana. Ghana National Museum, Accra.
(Right) Goldweight in the shape of a chameleon. Brass. Ashanti, Ghana. Length: 3⅝". Courtesy Museum of Primitive Art.

99 Covered vessel (*kuduo*). Brass. Ashanti, Ghana. Height: 15¾". The British Museum.

100 Chief's stool. Wood and metal. Ashanti, Ghana. Height: 14⅝". Courtesy Museum of Primitive Art.

101 Three designs of Ashanti stools, Ghana.

102 Queen mother's stool. Wood plated with silver. Ashanti, Ghana. Height: 16". The British Museum.

103 (Left) Chief's chair, decorated with brass nails. Ashanti, Ghana.
(Right) Three linguists' staffs. Gilded wood. Ghana.

104 Ashanti ruler in procession. Photo: Ghana Information Services.

105 Two handles of fly whisks. Wood. Baule, Ivory Coast. Height (l. to r.): 13½"; 10¾". Collection C. Price. Photo: Sandi Olivo.

106 Handle of fly whisk. Wood. Agni, Ivory Coast. Height: 13¾". Courtesy Museum of Primitive Art.

107 (Left) Gong beater. Wood. Baule, Ivory Coast. Height: 10¼". Courtesy Museum of Primitive Art.
(Right) Scepter. Wood plated with silver. Fon, Abomey, Dahomey. Height: 24⅞". Courtesy Museum of Primitive Art.

108 Gong and striker. Ivory. Benin, Nigeria, probably 1550–1650. Height of gong: 14¼". Length of striker: 11". The British Museum.

109 (Left) Drum and stand. Wood. Southern Baga, Guinea. Height: 44½". The British Museum.
(Right) Cup. Ivory. Benin, Nigeria, probably 1550–1650. Height: 7¾". University Museum, University of Pennsylvania.

110 House-post carved by Arowogun of Osi, 1919. Wood. Yoruba, Nigeria. Height: 41". Nigerian Museum, Lagos.

111 Palace doors by Arowogun of Osi. Wood. Yoruba, Nigeria. Height: 114". The British Museum.

112 Doors from the Palace at Ikere-Ekiti by Olowe of Ise. Wood. Yoruba, Nigeria. Height: 82". The British Museum.

113 Bandele, a Yoruba woodcarver, at work. Photo: Kevin Carroll.

114 Mask. Wood, paint, and fiber. Ibibio, Nigeria. Height: 22⅜". Courtesy Museum of Primitive Art.

115 (Left) Cult figure, probably representing a woman official of a secret society, with bowl for "medicine." Wood. Mende, Sierra Leone. Height: 17½". University Museum, University of Pennsylvania.

(Right) Bowl for palm nuts, for use in Fa divination. Wood. Fon, Dahomey, 19th century. Height: 7". The British Museum.

116 Bowl for Fa divination. Wood. Fon, Dahomey. Height: 8½". The Herskovits Collection. Photo: Frank Willett.

117 Yoruba diviner (babalawo) and his equipment at Ife, Nigeria. Photo: William Bascom.

118 Divination tray (opon ifa) and tapper (iro ifa). Wood. Yoruba, Nigeria. Size of tray: 11¾" x 12½". Length of tapper: 12". Collection C. Price. Photo: Sandi Olivo.

119 (Left) Pair of divination tappers. Wood. Fon, Dahomey. Height (l. to r.): 11"; 11⅝". Collections Jeannette Mirsky and C. Price. Photo: Sandi Olivo.

(Right) Ibeji figure. Wood with metal bracelets and beads. Yoruba, Nigeria, 19th century. Height: 10". Linden Museum, Stuttgart. Photo: Frank Willett.

120 (Left) Fertility doll (Akua-ba). Wood, seeds, and beads. Ashanti, Ghana. Height: 10¾". Courtesy Museum of Primitive Art.

(Right) Small figure. Wood. Ibo, Nigeria. Height: 6½". The British Museum.

121 Standing figure. Wood. Baule. Ivory Coast. Height: 20½". The British Museum.

122 Funerary screen. Wood and cane. Ijo, Nigeria, 19th century. Height: 36". The British Museum.

123 "Lady of Brass." Wood. Ijo, Nigeria, 19th century. Height: 33". University Museum, University of Pennsylvania.

124 Ikenga shrine. Wood. Ibo, Nigeria. Height: 19¾". The British Museum.

125 Ejiri figure. Wood. Ijo, Nigeria. Height: 27½". The British Museum.

126 Two stages in the carving of a dance wand for Shango by the carver Duga. Yoruba, Nigeria. Photos: William Bascom.

127 (Left) Duga painting the dance wand. Photo: William Bascom.

(Right) Dance wand with figure of a worshiper of Ifa. Wood. Yoruba, Oyo, Nigeria. Height: 21". Collection C. Price. Photo: Aldo Merusi.

128 (Left) Epa mask. Wood. Yoruba, Nigeria. The British Museum.

(Right) Mask. Wood. Dan, Ivory Coast or Liberia. Height: 21". University Museum, University of Pennsylvania.

129 (Left) Headpiece representing the elephant spirit of violence and ugliness. Wood. Ibo, Nigeria. Height: 15½". The British Museum.

(Right) Helmet mask, worn by women, leaders of the Bundu society. Wood and raffia. Mende, Sierra Leone. Height: 13¾". Courtesy Museum of Primitive Art.

130 (Left) Horned headpiece. Wood and animal skin. Ekoi, Nigeria. Height: 30½". The British Museum.

(Right) Antelope mask. Used in dances of the Zamle society. Wood. Guro, Ivory Coast. Height: 18¾". The British Museum.

131 (Top) Water-spirit headdress. Used in dances of the Ekine society. Wood and cartridge shells. Ijo, Nigeria. Length: 35¼". Courtesy Museum of Primitive Art.

(Bottom) Mask of ancestral spirit. Wood. Ibibio, Nigeria. Height: 9½". The British Museum.

132 Gelede mask. Wood and paint. Yoruba, Ketu, Dahomey. Height: 11¼". UCLA Museum of Cultural History, Gift of Mr. and Mrs. Harry Hughes.

133 Mask of Efe in the Gelede dance. Yoruba, Nigeria. Photo: Henry Drewal.

134 Screen by Adebisi Akanji for Esso Service Station, Oshogbo, Nigeria. Cement. Photo: Marshall W. Mount.

135 "The Awakening" by Ben Enwonwu. Bronze. Nigerian Museum, Lagos. Photo: Marshall W. Mount.

137 "Pregnant Mother and Child" (detail) by Vincent Kofi. Wood. Ghana. Photo: Marshall W. Mount.

138 Relief panel by Osagie Osifo. Wood. Catholic Chapel at the University of Ibadan, Nigeria. Photo: Kevin Carroll.

139 "Creation" by Tijani Mayakiri. Woodblock print. Ife, Nigeria. Photo: Sandi Olivo.

140 "Awakening Africa" by Vincent Kofi. Bronze. Collection of the artist. Photo: Marshall W. Mount.

Books for Further Reading

William R. Bascom and Paul Gebauer, *Handbook of West African Art*. Milwaukee Public Museum Handbook 5, Milwaukee, Wis., 1953.

Ulli Beier, *Art in Nigeria 1960*. Cambridge University Press, London, 1960.

————, *Contemporary Art in Africa*. Praeger, New York, 1968.

Jacqueline Delange, *The Art and Peoples of Black Africa* (trans. by Carol F. Jopling). Dutton, New York, 1974.

William Fagg, *Divine Kingship in Africa*. The Trustees of the British Museum, London, 1970. (On the art of Benin)

William Fagg and Margaret Plass, *African Sculpture*. Studio Vista, London, and Dutton Paperback, New York, 1964.

René Gardi, *African Crafts and Craftsmen*. Van Nostrand Reinhold, New York, 1969.

Louise E. Jefferson, *The Decorative Arts of Africa*. The Viking Press, New York, 1973.

Kate P. Kent, *Introducing West African Cloth*. Denver Museum of Natural History, Denver, Colo., 1971.

A. A. Y. Kyerematen, *Panoply of Ghana*. Praeger, New York, 1964.

Marshall W. Mount, *African Art: The Years Since 1920*. Indiana University Press, Bloomington, Ind., 1973.

Penelope Naylor, *Black Images: The Art of West Africa*. Doubleday, New York, 1973.

Boris de Rachewiltz, *Introduction to African Art*. John Murray, London, 1966.

Roy Sieber, *African Textiles and Decorative Arts*. The Museum of Modern Art, New York, 1972.

Robert F. Thompson, *Black Gods and Kings: Yoruba Art at UCLA*. University of California, Los Angeles, 1971.

Frank Willett, *African Art*. Praeger, New York, 1971.

————, *Ife in the History of West African Sculpture*. McGraw-Hill, New York, 1967.

Index

Italic number indicates illustration